A
PICTURE HISTORY
OF
CANADA

CLARKE HUTTON

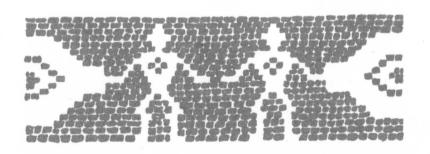

OXFORD UNIVERSITY PRESS
TORONTO

Oxford University Press, Amen House, Toronto
LONDON GLASGOW NEW YORK MELBOURNE WELLINGTON
BOMBAY CALCUTTA MADRAS KARACHI CAPE TOWN IBADAN
Geoffrey Cumberlege, Publisher to the University

First published 1956

Text written by
IVON OWEN and WILLIAM TOYE

DRAWN DIRECT TO THE PLATE BY CLARKE HUTTON AND LITHOGRAPHED
IN GREAT BRITAIN BY JESSE BROAD & CO. LTD., MANCHESTER
BOUND IN CANADA BY McCORQUODALE AND BLADES (CANADA) LIMITED

Eskimos

Bush
Indians

Bush Indians

Bush Indians

Longhouse Indians

THE FIRST CANADIANS

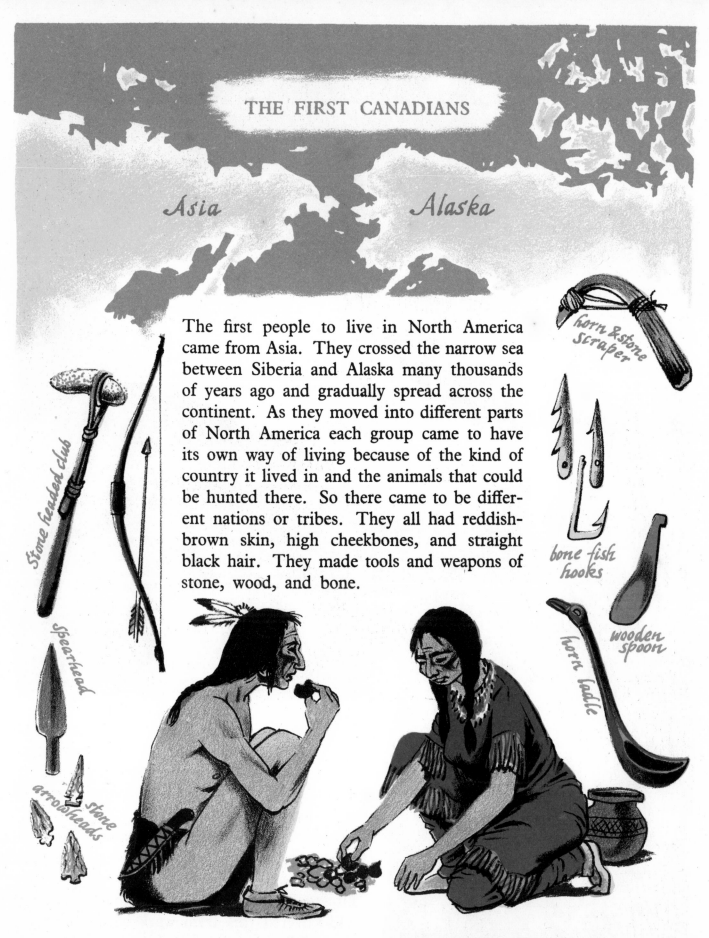

Asia

Alaska

horn & stone scraper

Stone headed club

The first people to live in North America came from Asia. They crossed the narrow sea between Siberia and Alaska many thousands of years ago and gradually spread across the continent. As they moved into different parts of North America each group came to have its own way of living because of the kind of country it lived in and the animals that could be hunted there. So there came to be different nations or tribes. They all had reddish-brown skin, high cheekbones, and straight black hair. They made tools and weapons of stone, wood, and bone.

bone fish hooks

wooden spoon

Spearhead

horn ladle

stone arrowheads

When Columbus found America he called the people he met Indians because he thought he had reached the Indies on the east coast of Asia. Though he was mistaken, they have been called Indians ever since.

1

Hunters of the Bush

From the Atlantic shore of eastern Canada to the western side of Hudson Bay stretched thousands of miles of rough, rocky country. It was covered by a thick forest of evergreens and birches — 'the bush'. Deer and moose lived there, and bears and wolves. In the thousands of rivers and lakes were beavers and many fish.

The Indians of the bush were hunters and fishermen. As they grew no crops they never settled long in one place but roamed about in small bands. They chose the best hunters as their leaders.

For shelter they used wigwams that could be set up quickly. Usually they took a number of poles and stuck them in the ground in a circle. They leant them together at the top and covered this framework with birchbark. Sometimes they bent the poles over so that the top of the wigwam was curved instead of pointed.

2

Their roads were the rivers and lakes. They travelled on them in canoes made of light wood covered with birchbark. The birchbark canoe was so well designed that a good paddler could handle it in very rough water, and so light that one or two men could carry it. If it was damaged, it was quickly repaired with a fresh sheet of bark taken from a near-by birch.

In winter when the waterways were frozen the Indians walked along them on snowshoes. Their clothes were made of moose or caribou skin. In winter they wore fur robes and jackets made from the skins of beavers and rabbits which they trapped.

The Longhouse Indians

Around Lake Ontario and Lake Erie lived the Longhouse nations. They grew some of their food — Indian corn, squash, pumpkins, and beans — and so they did not wander about but lived in villages surrounded by fields. Their longhouses were made of arched willow boughs covered with elm-bark. Each held several families and could be made longer to hold more. The villages were protected by palisades.

The women worked in the fields while the men hunted, fished, or gathered wild rice from the marshes. They used cooking-pots made of baked clay. Their clothes were usually made of deerskin. They travelled mostly on foot along forest trails. When they went on the water it was usually in canoes made from logs hollowed out by fire and scraped with stones and shells. Sometimes they made elm-bark canoes which were better than the log dug-outs but not nearly as good as birchbark canoes.

Each nation was ruled by a council of chosen village leaders called sachems. Five of the Longhouse nations made a solemn promise to work together and never to fight each other and these were called the League of Five Nations or the Iroquois. The strongest of the Five Nations were the Mohawks who lived mostly to the south of the St Lawrence River.

The Hurons, who lived near Georgian Bay on Lake Huron, did not join the League. This made the Iroquois their bitter enemies.

The Plains Indians

West of the rocky bush-country lie the flat prairies where great herds of bison or wild buffalo used to wander. The Plains Indians moved about the prairies following these herds. They hunted the buffalo for food and clothing.

Their shelters were tepees made of poles covered with buffalo hides. They were easily carried from place to place.

Their clothes were made of buffalo hide, often decorated with patterns of coloured porcupine-quills. On great occasions men wore flowing head-dresses of coloured feathers. Each feather stood for a brave deed the wearer had performed. Sometimes the head-dress was so long it trailed on the ground.

In early days they travelled on foot, using dogs to carry their supplies. But before they ever saw a white man they had learned to ride horses which had wandered north from the Spanish settlement in Mexico.

On the rivers they sometimes used tub-shaped boats covered with buffalo hide.

The Eskimos

In the far north lived the Eskimos. They were fishermen, seal-hunters, and caribou-hunters. Their summer tents were made of skins. In the long winters they lived in huts built of driftwood if they could find any, for there were no trees in their country. Otherwise they lived in igloos, made of blocks of hard snow.

The Eskimo canoe is called a kayak and is almost impossible to sink. It is made of whalebone completely covered with sealskin, except for a hole in which the paddler sits.

On land the Eskimos travelled by snowshoes or on sleighs pulled by teams of huskies, the Eskimo dogs.

Their clothes were made of caribou fur and sealskin.

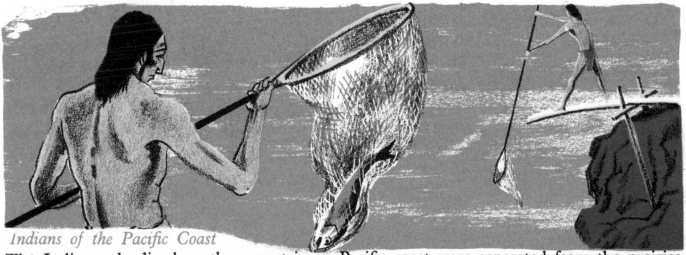

Indians of the Pacific Coast

The Indians who lived on the mountainous Pacific coast were separated from the prairies by the great Rocky Mountains. They lived chiefly on sea fish and the salmon of the rivers. They were not wandering people. Their villages lay along the coast or on the many islands off it.

Some of their clothes were woven of wool taken from mountain goats and other animals.

Very tall trees grow in this region. The Indians cut planks from fallen cedars to build their big houses. Their canoes were hollowed-out cedar logs, which they shaped by steaming the wood so as to soften it enough to be stretched.

They liked to decorate the things they used by carving and painting them. They believed that certain animals and birds were their ancestors, and these were their favourite subjects. After they obtained metal tools from the white men they were able to carve these creatures on huge totem poles. A totem pole stood in front of a great man's house to show his noble ancestry, rather like a coat of arms.

Unlike other Canadian Indians, the Pacific Indians were ruled by hereditary chiefs, and thought wealth and ancestry very important. They vied with each other in giving great feasts called potlatches at which the host gave away his possessions to his guests. Much of their work was done by slaves, who were prisoners captured in battle.

Many people think of the Indians as fierce and cruel. Some of them were, sometimes. But more often they were peaceful.

In Canada the Indians did not fight against the coming of the white men. They helped the explorers by showing them where to go and teaching them to live and travel in the forest. They gave them the snowshoe and the toboggan, and — best of all — the birchbark canoe, that beautiful boat that made the exploration of North America possible.

THE DISCOVERERS

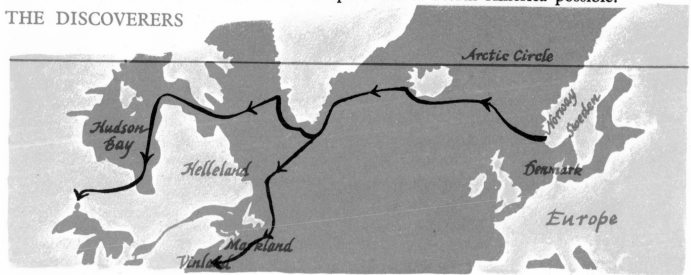

The first white men to see North America were probably Vikings. These daring sailors from Norway, Sweden, and Denmark colonized Iceland in the North Atlantic over a thousand years ago and then started a settlement in Greenland. One of their ships lost its way on the voyage from Iceland to Greenland and sighted a strange land. When the sailors got home and told their story a Viking named Leif the Lucky decided to explore the unknown country. He landed in three places, which he named Helleland (rocky country), Markland (forest country), and Vinland (grapevine country). These may have been Labrador, Nova Scotia, and New England. Other Vikings must have reached northern Ontario by way of Hudson Bay. We know this because a rusted Viking sword has lately been found there.

Nobody else tried to discover what lay across the Atlantic until Columbus found the West Indies nearly five hundred years later.

In 1497 John Cabot sailed west from the English port of Bristol. The first land he saw he named 'the New-Found-Land'. There were so many fish in the shallow sea off Newfoundland — the 'Grand Banks' — that the sailors caught them in baskets. Cabot landed on Cape Breton Island and claimed it for King Henry VII of England.

The English were more interested in the fish he had found than in the land. They made no colony, but from then on fishermen crossed the Atlantic every summer to catch cod on the Grand Banks.

Fishermen came from other countries too — from France, Spain, and Portugal. Sometimes they met Indians on the shore and traded knives or beads for furs.

THE FOUNDING OF NEW FRANCE

After a time the king of France sent Jacques Cartier to explore the new land. In 1535 he sailed up the St Lawrence River. He landed where the city of Quebec now stands and found an Iroquois village called Stadacona. The Indians were friendly. They pointed up the river and said 'Canada', a word whose Indian meaning we do not know. Cartier thought it must be the name of the country. He sailed on up the river until he came to a place where rapids barred his way and he landed on a large island. There, beside an Indian village called Hochelaga, was a high hill which Cartier named Mount Royal — in French, *Mont Réal*.

Cartier and his men spent a long, cold winter near Stadacona. As they had no fresh food and ate little more than salt pork, they fell ill with scurvy. They learned of an Indian cure — spruce-bark tea — but not before twenty-five had died.

10

For many years no lasting colony was established on the St Lawrence. But fishermen kept coming over and bringing back furs as well as fish to sell in Europe. They were able to get high prices for the furs, especially when the beaver hat became fashionable for men. The king of France saw then that the new country could be useful, and he gave a nobleman named de Monts a monopoly on the fur trade. This meant that only men who worked for him could trade with the Indians. In return he was to start a colony. De Monts decided to try Acadia (what we now call the Maritime Provinces) for his colony because it was further south than the St Lawrence and might not have such hard winters.

In 1604, therefore, de Monts, another nobleman named Poutrincourt, and Samuel de Champlain, the king's geographer, took two ships up the Bay of Fundy to an island in the St Croix River. They started a settlement there. But the island lacked wood and fresh water, and after a hard winter they moved across the Bay of Fundy to a place which they named Port Royal.

There the men started a farm. They hunted in the surrounding woods and fished in the rivers. Champlain worked at making maps of the country.

They formed a club, the Order of Good Cheer, which gave them amusement during the long winter evenings.

But other Frenchmen wanted to join in the fur trade, and they complained to the king about de Monts's monopoly. In the spring of their second year, the settlers at Port Royal received the news that the monopoly was cancelled. Discouraged, they went home. A few years later Poutrincourt and his sons came back. By this time the English were starting colonies further south on the Atlantic coast and wanted Acadia too. So began the first of many attacks on Port Royal.

Meanwhile de Monts had persuaded the king to give him a monopoly of the St Lawrence fur trade for one more year. In 1608 Champlain landed at the place on the river that the Indians called Kebec. There, in front of a high cliff, he put up three buildings and laid out a garden. This little trading post was to grow into the city of Quebec.

The next summer Champlain went with a band of friendly Indians to help them fight against the Iroquois. The Iroquois were startled by Champlain's guns and fled.

Champlain travelled by canoe up the Ottawa River. One year he made his way through the rivers and lakes of the northern bush and looked for the first time on the vast expanse of Lake Huron — 'the Freshwater Sea' as he called it. The canoe route he followed became known as 'the Champlain Road'.

Quebec's first colonist was Louis Hébert, who brought his wife and children to Canada in 1617. He built a stone house on top of the cliff, cleared his land of trees, and started to raise crops and animals. Because he had been a druggist in France, he served as Quebec's doctor.

Champlain sent for missionaries to teach the Indians about Christianity. Most of the missionaries who came were Jesuit priests. The most famous of them was Father Brébeuf. The priests went to live in the Huron villages. They learned the Huron language, preached, and baptized many Indians. Some went long distances by canoe to preach to other Indian nations, and explored much of the country round the Great Lakes.

The Jesuits described their life among the Indians in reports which they sent to France once a year to be printed. Many people who read of their adventures and hardships wanted to help these brave men. Some gave money; others decided to go to New France and join in the work. Maisonneuve, a soldier, led a party of about fifty people to the island of Montreal in the St Lawrence, where they built houses, a mission, and a hospital. They called this little settlement Ville-Marie. It was the beginning of the city of Montreal.

The following December a winter flood threatened to destroy Ville-Marie. Maisonneuve vowed that if the settlement was spared he would carry a wooden cross up the steep slope of Mount Royal and plant it at the summit as a token of his gratitude. Ville-Marie was unharmed and Maisonneuve did as he had promised.

Montreal quickly became important for trade, since it stood where the Ottawa River joined the St Lawrence. Each year in the early summer fleets of Indian canoes came down the rivers from the Great Lakes and the northern bush to attend the fur fair at Ville-Marie. Here the Indians traded beaver pelts for cloth, knives, and hatchets.

The Hurons, living on the edge of the fur country, guarded the trade routes to the

St Lawrence. The Iroquois wanted to get northern furs to sell to Dutch traders living in their country. So Iroquois war parties began to raid the Huron villages.

The Jesuits decided to build a fortified headquarters for their mission. They called it Sainte-Marie-among-the-Hurons. It had thirteen buildings, a large farm, and even a canal. One year Sainte-Marie sheltered and fed six thousand Indians.

But the Iroquois, armed with Dutch guns, kept growing stronger and fiercer. In a great raid in 1649 they burnt villages and crops, slaughtered the Hurons, and tortured and killed two missionaries, one of whom was Father Brébeuf. The Jesuits themselves set fire to Sainte-Marie rather than let the Iroquois capture it. In two years only three hundred of the once-powerful Huron nation were left.

The Iroquois grew bolder. With the Hurons gone, the Montreal fur trade almost stopped. Iroquois warriors began to steal into Ville-Marie to kill unwary townsmen. In 1660 young Adam Dollard volunteered to ambush as many Iroquois as he could find on the Ottawa River. With sixteen men he went up the river to the swirling waters of the Long Sault rapids, where forty Hurons and Algonquins joined him beside a deserted stockade. There they waited.

In a few days the stockade was surrounded by over seven hundred Iroquois. They were stopped by a fire of gunshot every time they approached it. The days passed but the courageous Frenchmen continued to hold them off. Then Dollard's water supply began to give out; his Huron allies deserted to the enemy. On the ninth day the Iroquois, carrying lighted torches and rough wooden shields, moved toward the stockade. With screeching war cries they climbed over it, set fire to the logs, and killed the seventeen Frenchmen.

It had taken over seven hundred Iroquois eight days and nights to defeat Dollard and his small band. Iroquois confidence was shaken by this fight; they never attacked Ville-Marie.

NEW FRANCE AND ITS RIVALS

Until now New France had been governed by a company. The colony was not growing fast because the company was interested in furs, not in farms or towns. Then the king and his minister Colbert decided to end company rule. The king appointed a Governor, and an Intendant to run business affairs. These two, with Bishop Laval who was the Pope's representative in Canada, were to govern New France under the king.

But first twelve hundred French soldiers were sent out. In one swift blow they brought ruin to the Iroquois villages. For a time Canada had peace.

Jean Talon, the first intendant, knew that what Canada needed most was people. He attracted many settlers by promising them grants of land, and free food and clothing until their first crop was harvested. He made laws to encourage men to marry and have large families, and since there were few women in the colony he sent home for shiploads of young women to be wives for the settlers. King Louis gave each one who would go a wedding gift of money.

Land in New France was divided into great estates granted by the king to *seigneurs* or lords. These men promised to settle people on their estates and to fight for the king when needed. Each *seigneur* rented most of his land to *habitants* — farmers who cleared the trees from their lots, planted crops, and raised animals.

The main highway was a river — the St Lawrence. It was travelled by snowshoe and sleigh in winter and by boat in summer. Most *habitants* wanted to live on the river, so their farms were arranged in long, narrow strips running back from the water. They lived in whitewashed stone or wood houses, built close together for companionship.

The *habitant* worked hard. He produced all his food himself, from the soil, the river, or the forest. He built his own house, his two-wheeled cart, his sleigh, and even his furniture. He wore clothes of homespun cloth, and his furs and leather came from his skill at trapping and shooting.

On St Martin's day in November the *habitant* families gathered at the great house of the *seigneur* and paid him their rent, which might be ten or twelve sous, a bushel of grain, a pig, or a few chickens.

The *curé* or priest, who preached to them on Sundays and feast days, was their friend and counsellor throughout the week. The village church was the centre of their lives.

In winter they had time to hunt, to race in their horsedrawn sleighs on the frozen river, and to gather in each other's houses. They loved to dance to the tune of a fiddle, to sing their folksongs, such as 'Alouette', and to tell stories that have been handed down from parents to children until the present day.

Now that Quebec was the capital of a royal province, a social life of colourful balls and stately ceremonies grew up at the governor's court.

In the late summer and fall Quebec was thronged with people who came to watch the arrival of ships from France. The port hummed with excitement as bales of costly materials and clothes in the latest fashion were unloaded and sold to those who could afford them.

But many Frenchmen preferred the adventure of Indian life and the thrill of seeing country where no white man had been before. They were called *coureurs de bois* or 'vagabonds of the bush'. They lived in the forest, sometimes sharing the smoke-filled shelters of Indians, sometimes sleeping out in the open on beds of fir-boughs. Every spring their canoes swept down to Montreal loaded with furs. Before summer they disappeared into the wilderness again, their canoes this time laden with trade goods and food, their paddles flashing to the rhythm of a rollicking song.

Two *coureurs*, Pierre Radisson and Chouart de Groseilliers, were the first white men to explore the country west of Lake Superior and, in 1663, to reach Hudson Bay by land. From this trip they returned with a fleet of 360 canoes loaded with furs. But they had no licence to trade and were heavily fined. Angrily they went to England and told Prince Rupert of the rich northern fur country. The prince was so impressed that he and some English merchants formed a company of ' Gentlemen Adventurers trading into Hudson's Bay ' — the Hudson's Bay Company. It claimed the right to trade in all land whose waters flow into Hudson Bay — nearly a million square miles which the Company named Rupert's Land.

La Salle

Prince Rupert

Robert Cavelier de la Salle was a *seigneur* who believed that he could find a way through North America to Asia. He talked of this idea so much that he was nicknamed ' *Sieur de la Chine* ' — Lord of China — and the place where his seigneury was is still called Lachine. La Salle was determined to explore the West and claim it for France before the English could get there.

22

One day in 1679 the Indians at the Jesuit Mission of Michilimackinac, at the head of Lake Huron, saw an amazing sight. A stately ship sailed into their bay — the first ever seen on the Upper Lakes. Her name was the *Griffon*. La Salle had built her on the Niagara River and had now brought her safely through a furious gale on the Freshwater Sea. As she approached the Mission, her five guns fired a salute. And while the ship lay at anchor surrounded by a hundred canoes, La Salle and his men paraded to the little bark chapel to give thanks for their safe arrival.

La Salle pressed into the interior of the continent on foot and by canoe and at last followed the mighty Mississippi River to its mouth. He named the land here Louisiana after the king. The French Empire now stretched from the Gulf of St Lawrence to the Gulf of Mexico.

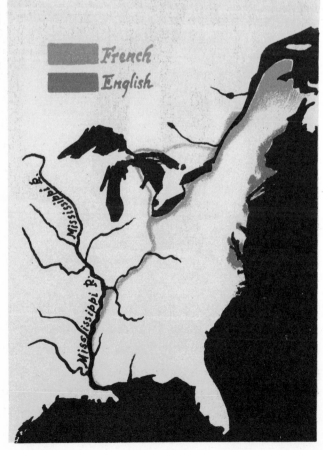

French
English

Meanwhile Count de Frontenac, who had become governor in 1672, was strengthening the defences of New France. He had La Salle invite the Iroquois to meet him at Cataraqui at the head of the St Lawrence where Kingston now stands. The governor arrived at the meeting with a dazzling flotilla of troops — 120 scarlet-and-gold canoes bearing uniformed officers and men, and two flatboats armed with cannons. Like a great king he gave audience to the Iroquois sachems. He told them that he was building a fort there and asked for their good will.

The Iroquois were filled with awe and respect for the 'Great Onontio', as they called Frontenac. Up to then they had been crossing the river at Cataraqui to trade with the English. When Fort Frontenac was built they started to trade with the French there. War broke out between England and France in 1688. This meant fighting in America — in Acadia, which the New Englanders wanted, in Newfoundland where there were both French and English settlements, and in the North-West where the French wanted to drive out the Hudson's Bay traders.

Frontenac led an expedition against the New England villages. The New Englanders replied by capturing Port Royal. Then Sir William Phips took a fleet to Quebec and demanded its surrender. Frontenac haughtily defied him. The English guns were useless against the high cliff, and the fleet sailed away.

In the North-West the French captured many Hudson's Bay Company posts. Later on La Vérendrye built forts in what is now Manitoba. His sons were the first white men to cross the prairies as far as the foothills of the Rocky Mountains.

Port Royal was handed back to the French in a treaty, but was captured again by the English in 1710. They renamed it Annapolis Royal and Acadia became the British province of Nova Scotia or New Scotland. The British government offered free land to everyone who would come out to start a colony. Farmers, sailors, carpenters, masons, blacksmiths, and engineers answered the call. In a matter of months a town arose on one of the finest harbours in the world. It was called Halifax. But the Acadians were not happy. Six thousand of them refused to swear loyalty to the British king, so they were put on ships and sent away — expelled from the land they had cleared and tilled, their homes destroyed. In 1735 the first road was opened between Quebec and Montreal. It took a carriage four and a half days to travel from one town to the other.

In 1756 war broke out between Britain and France again. Pitt, the British prime minister, determined to end the French empire in America. He sent a young general, James Wolfe, to capture Quebec. France sent the gallant Marquis de Montcalm to defend it.

Wolfe's army camped across the river from Quebec. For months it seemed impossible to overcome the fortress on its high cliff. Then one of Wolfe's men noticed some women washing clothes in the river and later saw the clothes drying at the top of the cliff; so he knew there must be a path to the top. One dark night in September 1759 Wolfe and forty-five hundred men crossed the river to the little bay now called Wolfe's Cove and crept up the path. At dawn the watchers in the city were startled to see the British army drawn up on the Plains of Abraham. The French troops rushed out to meet them. In two hours the fight was over. The British won, but Wolfe was killed on the battlefield. Soon after, Montcalm died of his wounds. The British flag was raised over Quebec.

In 1763 France signed a treaty acknowledging that New France now belonged to Britain. It was renamed the Province of Quebec.

Few English-speaking settlers came into the new province, but some traders did come to the towns. They wanted the colony to be governed like other British colonies. But the governor felt that this would be unfair to the French-Canadians. They were allowed to keep their laws, their religion, and their language.

BRITISH NORTH AMERICA

By 1763 the Hudson's Bay Company had seven forts on Hudson Bay and James Bay. The Indians living near those forts brought them furs and buffalo hides that they had bought from the Plains Indians. The traders themselves seldom went inland.

Now that Canada was British, the Company faced a new challenge — 'the Pedlars'. These were English and Scottish adventurers who thrust into the interior of Rupert's Land with the help of French-Canadian *coureurs de bois* and *voyageurs* — canoemen skilled at handling huge freight-canoes in the turbulent rivers and broad lakes of the interior.

These independent traders set up a head-quarters at Grand Portage on Lake Superior and from there scattered across the prairies and into the valleys of the Saskatchewan and Athabaska rivers. They built their trading posts in places that would be passed by Indians on their way to the Company forts; so the Indians often sold their furs at these posts instead of to the Company.

By this time the thirteen colonies down the Atlantic coast felt ready to run their own affairs and fought to become an independent nation. An American army captured Montreal. But when they found that the Canadians would not rebel with them they went home.

The Americans won their independence in 1781. The new country was called the United States of America.

There were people in the United States who wanted to remain British. About forty thousand of them accepted an offer of free land and provisions in Nova Scotia and Quebec. They were called United Empire Loyalists. Ships left New York carrying thousands of Loyalists to Nova Scotia — aristocrats with their Negro slaves, merchants, farmers, teachers, doctors, and engineers. They settled in established towns like Halifax and Annapolis Royal; they began new towns like Shelburne, Digby, and Parrtown (later Saint John); and they cleared forests to start farms on Cape Breton and Prince Edward Island, now a separate province. So many people settled on the north shore of the Bay of Fundy that another new province was formed — New Brunswick, with Fredericton as its capital.

Parts shaded red show United Empire Loyalist settlements

Other Loyalists, mostly farmers, moved into Quebec. They went chiefly to the uninhabited western part of the province, and cleared land on the north shore of the upper St Lawrence and Lake Ontario. Still more settled on the Niagara Peninsula. Indian Loyalists, the Mohawks, settled in the valley of the Grand River under their leader Joseph Brant.

A few government tools and their bare hands were all the Loyalists had to help them win new homes from the wilderness. Trees had to be cut down, a cabin built, furniture made, stumps pulled, the ground dug, hoed, and planted. Two enemies hindered them — cold and hunger — but hardship was met with courage.

The pioneers helped each other in gatherings called bees. Together, neighbours did in a day what one family would have taken weeks to do. They had bees for house-raising, logging, ploughing — even for quilting and apple-paring. Bees gave them fun as well as work, for after the job was finished they celebrated with a feast and dancing.

The Loyalists in western Quebec did not want to live under French laws. In 1791, therefore, the province (now named Canada) was divided into Upper Canada — the part west of the Ottawa River — and Lower Canada where the French-Canadians lived.

The first capital of Upper Canada was Niagara-on-the-Lake. There, in September 1792, in a colourful ceremony, Lieutenant-Governor Simcoe opened the Assembly — Upper Canada's first parliament.

This was the first legislature in the British Empire to pass a law forbidding slavery.

Niagara was too close to the American border, and two years later Simcoe founded a new town on the north shore of Lake Ontario, to be the capital of Upper Canada. Its name was York.

Three fur-traders, the Frobisher brothers and Simon Fraser, thought it would be easier to compete with the Hudson's Bay Company in the huge North-West if all the independent traders united. The North West Company was formed in 1783. Its members were called 'the Nor' Westers' to distinguish them from 'the Gentlemen' of the Hudson's Bay Company.

Every spring the chiefs of the new Company travelled from Montreal to Grand Portage and Fort William. *Voyageurs* took the traders and supplies up the Ottawa, across to Georgian Bay by the Champlain Road, and on to the Upper Lakes. The canoes travelled in brigades, sometimes thirty to a brigade. When they came to a waterfall or had to go from one river to another, everyone walked and carried the canoes and supplies. This was called a portage.

Traders who had spent the winter scattered over thousands of miles of wilderness came to Fort William to report. They received supplies and trade goods for the coming year, and had their furs checked and sent back to Montreal.

The Nor' Westers explored new country. In 1789 Alexander Mackenzie went down the mighty river that flows out of Great Slave Lake, hoping that it ran to the western sea. We call it the Mackenzie River. Mackenzie named it River Disappointment, for it turned north after all and led him at last to the ice-filled Arctic Ocean.

Mackenzie next decided to cross the Rocky Mountains to the Pacific. In the spring of 1793 he and his *voyageurs* paddled up the Peace River into the mountains. Sometimes they had to tow their canoe up foaming rapids, clinging to steep cliffs while they did so. When they portaged they had to cut their way through thick forest. They met Indians who threw rocks and shot arrows at them.

They crossed the Rockies and at last reached the Bella Coola River, where friendly Indians gave Mackenzie a dug-out canoe to carry him to the sea. On 22 July he reached the coast and proudly painted his name on a rock — 'Alex Mackenzie from Canada by land' — the first white man to complete the journey.

In 1804 The North West Company sent Simon Fraser to open trading posts beyond the Rockies. In 1808, with ten *voyageurs* he paddled through the canyons and over the rapids and whirlpools of the turbulent river that now bears his name.

David Thompson was a great geographer who surveyed the country west of the Great Lakes and made the first accurate maps of it. In 1811 he explored the Columbia River to its mouth and built trading posts in this area, known as the Oregon territory. The Americans, who had explored to the Pacific coast thirteen years after Mackenzie, were trading there too, but they soon yielded to the competition of the Nor' Westers.

At this time Britain was fighting against the French Emperor Napoleon. Britain angered the United States by searching American ships at sea to look for runaway British sailors. For this reason, and because many Americans thought that all North America should be under one flag, the United States declared war in 1812. The United States then had about six million citizens; there were only about half a million people in British North America.

The main American attack was against Upper Canada, where the leader of the defending forces was Sir Isaac Brock. He was helped by the Shawnee Indians, led by Tecumseh. General Brock captured Detroit. He was killed in the battle of Queenston Heights, but his men drove the Americans back across the Niagara River. Later, the Americans captured York. At Put-In Bay on Lake Erie Commodore Perry destroyed a British fleet.

By 1814 both sides were tired of the war. Peace was made, and since then all differences between the two countries have been settled by discussion.

Lord Selkirk, one of the owners of the Hudson's Bay Company, bought from the Company a large tract of rolling prairie land on the Red River. In 1811 he sent a group of needy settlers from the Scottish Highlands to start farms there. Fort Douglas was founded. This was the beginning of the city of Winnipeg.

These pioneers suffered from more than the usual hardships of building new homes in a strange land. The Nor' Westers thought that the colony was planned by the Hudson's Bay Company to interfere with their trading; and the Indians and Métis (half Indian and half French) were angry at seeing their hunting grounds turned into farms. Over the next few years there was fighting. Crops were destroyed, lives were lost, Fort Douglas was captured by the Nor' Westers. Peace was not restored until 1817.

In 1821 the long rivalry of the Nor' Westers and the Gentlemen was ended. The two companies united under one name — the Hudson's Bay Company, owners of half a continent.

The new governor of this vast territory was Sir George Simpson. He kept in touch with his men by visiting all the trading posts — from York Factory on Hudson Bay to Fort Vancouver on the Columbia, a distance of 2,600 miles. He travelled in a big red canoe that was made to go as fast as possible by a crew of the best *voyageurs*. Traders and Indians were deeply impressed when a brigade of Company canoes swept up to a fort. The *voyageurs* sang in time to the mighty strokes of their scarlet paddles, bagpipes sounded, flags fluttered in the wind; in the centre of the largest canoe sat Governor Simpson in a tall beaver hat, come for a tour of inspection.

Between 1815 and 1850 many changes took place in British North America. From England and Wales, Ireland, and Scotland, so many new settlers poured in that the population increased from half a million to nearly three million. Many of these people were very poor; they endured living in the dark and airless hold of a sailing ship for as long as eight weeks to become pioneers in a land of promise.

Some became lumbermen in the forests of the St Lawrence valley, the Ottawa valley, or New Brunswick. All winter they felled tall trees and dragged the square-hewn logs to the bank of the nearest river. When the ice melted in the spring the logs were bound together in huge rafts and floated downstream to the harbour of Quebec or Saint John.

The shores of the Maritimes were dotted with shipyards where great wooden vessels were built. The lumber, wheat, and fish produced by the pioneers were carried in these ships to the West Indies or across the Atlantic. The ships brought back clothes, machinery, sugar, tea, and tobacco.

The clipper ships of the 'Bluenose' seamen of Nova Scotia were famous for their speed and beauty.

Many people moved into the bushland of Upper Canada and the Maritimes to clear farms there. Some of them had never farmed before, but their hard work and the rich soil produced many thousands of bushels of wheat every year.

In Upper Canada, where people were turning the wilderness into farms and villages, roads were very important. Roads between villages were simply forest trails used by people on foot or horseback. The Dundas Highway, running east and west of York, and Yonge Street, running north, were hacked out of the forest by Governor Simcoe's men. They were full of mud-holes and tree-stumps and in wet weather were almost impossible to travel over. Logs were laid side by side over some roads to make them safer. It was a bumpy trip over these ' corduroy ' roads in a springless stage-coach or cart. The longest road linked Quebec, Montreal, Kingston, and York.

People in those days preferred to travel by water because it was smoother and safer, but it was far from comfortable. Passengers in Durham boats that travelled between Upper and Lower Canada sat on the open deck with the freight. Sometimes they had to get out and walk while the boat was dragged over rapids.

In 1817 the first steamship began to ply the Great Lakes. By the 1830's there were steamers even on the smaller lakes and rivers. Some of them were very luxurious.

In 1833 the *Royal William*, built at Quebec, was the first ship to cross the Atlantic under steam. A few years later Samuel Cunard of Halifax began a regular steamship service between Nova Scotia and Great Britain. This was the beginning of the famous Cunard Line.

In 1832 the Rideau Canal was completed. It connected the Ottawa River with Lake Ontario at Kingston. Where it joined the Ottawa a lumber town grew up, named Bytown after the man who directed the building of the canal. It later became the city of Ottawa.

By 1848 a chain of canals had been completed around the rapids of the upper St Lawrence, and the Welland Canal had been built to bypass Niagara Falls. Ships could then sail from the Atlantic to Lake Huron.

In 1834 the name of York (called 'muddy York' because of its bad roads) was changed to Toronto. It became the fifth city in British North America, along with Halifax, Saint John, Quebec, and Montreal.

Only those who could afford to pay for education attended the earliest pioneer schools. They were rude log buildings furnished with a few benches. There were no blackboards. Paper was scarce, so slates or sometimes pieces of birchbark were used as notebooks. Reading, writing, and arithmetic were the only subjects taught.

By the 1840's each province had a system of schools to which children could go without paying fees.

Many people in the Canadas and Nova Scotia wanted 'responsible government' — that is, government by a Cabinet that could be dismissed by the elected representatives of the people. These Reformers were bitterly opposed by the governors and the ruling families that surrounded them. In Lower Canada the Reformers were led by Louis Joseph Papineau, in Upper Canada by William Lyon Mackenzie. In 1837 there were riots in Montreal and Papineau was blamed. Soldiers sent into the countryside to arrest him were met by armed *habitants* and defeated. But after a few more battles the Lower Canada rebellion was crushed. The governor of Upper Canada sent all his troops to help in Lower Canada. Mackenzie then summoned his followers for an attack on Toronto. Volunteers marched out to meet them and after a twenty-minute battle (in which nobody was hurt) the rebels were scattered.

Mackenzie and Papineau fled to the United States. But their cause was won in the end. Britain sent Lord Durham, himself a Reformer, to find out what was wrong. As a result of his report, responsible government came at last — to Nova Scotia and the newly united province of Canada in 1848, and in the next seven years to Prince Edward Island, New Brunswick, and Newfoundland.

In 1846 the Oregon country was handed over to the United States. Fort Victoria, at the south end of Vancouver Island, then became the headquarters of the western fur trade. It was a sleepy settlement of log buildings and farms until gold was found on the mainland. Prospectors from the United States thronged into the interior. They went on foot and by pack mule through thick forest, across swaying Indian bridges, and along mountain precipices to look for gold in the sandbars of the Fraser River. Fort Victoria became a city of tents, a stopping-off place for gold-seekers.

In 1858 the mainland was made a separate colony, called British Columbia. A road 480 miles long was blasted through river canyons and around cliffs to the Cariboo country. Stagecoaches were soon thundering over the twisting, perilous road, carrying men who had walked and ridden across the continent or sailed round Cape Horn to get there.

Victoria, now a city, was made the capital of British Columbia when Vancouver Island joined the mainland colony. The fame of the Far West and its mild climate attracted many settlers. Lumbering and salmon-fishing industries began.

Meanwhile the eastern provinces were growing prosperous. They governed themselves, they traded freely with the United States and with each other. Railways were built, and seemed to shrink vast distances. Some men began to dream of joining the provinces into one country that might one day become a great nation — perhaps stretching from the Atlantic to the Pacific.

In 1864, at a meeting in Quebec, delegates from all five provinces discussed a union or confederation. A plan was drawn up to have a national parliament in which both English and French would be spoken, an assembly in each province, and a governor-general to keep the country linked to the British Crown. Newfoundland and Prince Edward Island decided not to join, but Canada, New Brunswick, and Nova Scotia went ahead with the idea. Their plan was put into the British North America Act.

THE NATION

The people of the three provinces looked forward with mounting excitement to the first of July, 1867. For 'on and after that day', said the Act, they were to 'form and be One Dominion under the name of Canada'.

All across the new country the day was brilliantly sunny. Everyone had a holiday. There were parades, picnics, and sports. In Ottawa, the capital, Sir John A. Macdonald, chief of the 'Fathers of Confederation', took office as the first Prime Minister of Canada. In the evening all the cities had great displays of fireworks.

There were now four provinces: Ontario (formerly Upper Canada), Quebec (Lower Canada), New Brunswick, and Nova Scotia.

Sir John A. Macdonald

The Red River colony was growing slowly. The Métis and the descendants of Selkirk's settlers farmed on the river and hunted.

Furs were transported five hundred miles south to St Paul, the westernmost point of the railway in the United States. Long lines of Red River carts, made entirely of wood, squeaked and rumbled their way back and forth between Fort Garry and St Paul.

In 1869 the Hudson's Bay Company sold its rights over Rupert's Land to Canada. It was renamed the Northwest Territories. Government surveyors arrived in the Red River district to lay out square land divisions and roads on the long, narrow farms. The Métis feared that they would lose their farms and their free life on the open prairie. Their leader, Louis Riel, wanted the district made a province of the Dominion so that his people could keep their language, land, and customs. When a lieutenant-governor arrived to take charge, Riel opposed him and set up his own government.

Riel ruled at Fort Garry for eight months, until the Dominion government made the settlement a province. It was called Manitoba. The Métis were given new land to farm. Many of them found that they did not like to live in a settled community, and moved west to the empty prairies around the North Saskatchewan River.

In 1871 the government formally obtained from the Indians the land that was Manitoba and the Northwest Territories. A thousand braves gathered to watch one member from each band sign a treaty with the Queen's representatives. The Indians accepted a yearly payment for their land — a payment that is kept up to this day and is to go on 'as long as the sun goes round and water flows'. They were given large reserves of land to live on.

The Northwest Mounted Police (later named the Royal Canadian Mounted Police) rode across the West to establish order and justice. Lawlessness was quickly punished. The Indians admired and trusted the Mounties in their scarlet tunics.

When Sir John A. Macdonald invited British Columbia to join Canada, the colony accepted on condition that a railway would be built from eastern Canada to the west coast. This was promised and in 1871 British Columbia became the sixth province in the Dominion. In 1873 Prince Edward Island also joined the confederation. Now all British North America, except Newfoundland, was in Canada.

In 1880 the Canadian Pacific Railway Company began Canada's first transcontinental railway.

It took five years to build. A team of thousands of men cut through the bush of northern Ontario and blasted a roadbed with dynamite along the rocky north shore of Lake Superior. Another worked on the prairies, laying over three miles of track a day. The third team, working east from the Pacific, laid tracks through the Kicking Horse Pass, on high trestle bridges, in tunnels passing through solid walls of rock, and along mountain ledges.

In November 1885 the two western teams met in the Rockies. When the final spike — a golden one — was driven in the last length of track, a country of only $4\frac{1}{2}$ million people had the longest railway in the world. Halifax and Vancouver were joined by an unbroken line of steel.

With a railway close to their new hunting ground, the Métis under Riel rebelled again. They were joined by a few Indians led by Big Bear and Poundmaker. But trains rushed soldiers to the spot and after a few fierce battles peace was restored.

The railway brought throngs of settlers to the empty prairies — people from eastern Canada, from the United States (whose western plains had filled up), and from Britain, Scandinavia, Finland, Russia, Poland, Germany, Austria, the Ukraine, and Italy. Settlers came as far as they could by train. Then each family hired an oxcart to carry their belongings, and walked beside it — sometimes for many days — over the rough, muddy trails to their allotment of land. These new settlers became wheat farmers, and the customs of their native lands came to be part of prairie life.

In a few years the fertile prairies turned into a vast rippling sea of wheat, green in spring and golden in summer. Tall, lonely grain elevators rose into the sky every few miles. They stored the wheat until it was shipped by rail to the Lakehead, through the Great Lakes in grain ships to the east, and then to countries all over the world.

The cities of Saskatoon, Regina, Calgary, and Edmonton grew up in what was once a prairie wilderness. The provinces of Alberta and Saskatchewan were created out of the North-west Territories in 1905.

The Yukon Territory was formed in 1898 after gold was discovered in Bonanza Creek, a tributary of the Klondike River. Edmonton became a boom-town where prospectors bought supplies before starting out with carts, pack horses, and dog teams to join the Gold Rush at Dawson City. The ballads of Robert W. Service made the rough, colourful life of the Klondike 'sourdoughs' famous everywhere.

Through most of these years the government was headed by Sir Wilfrid Laurier, the first French-Canadian prime minister of Canada. Poets were appearing to write of the land and its people — Louis Fréchette in French, Archibald Lampman and Bliss Carman in English. New railways opened up Northern Ontario, where a wealth of gold, silver, nickel, and copper was mined.

The powerful falls at Niagara and the swift-flowing rivers of Quebec were harnessed to generators that produced hydro-electric power. With electricity eastern factories made machinery, furniture, and clothing. Houses and city streets were lighted by electricity instead of gas.

In the Maritimes huge mills were built for changing iron into steel. Coal was mined on Cape Breton Island and apple orchards flourished in the Annapolis Valley.

In addition to lumber and salmon, British Columbia developed silver mines in the Kootenay district, and dairy and fruit farms in the Fraser valley. Vancouver was a busy port for trade with the Orient — and, once the Panama Canal was opened, with Europe. Southern Alberta had become grazing land for huge herds of cattle. Beef joined the growing number of exports. The cowboy, with his broad-brimmed hat, snug-fitting trousers, and high-heeled boots, became a familiar figure in the West. He drove the cattle to pasture and water, branded them at the round-up, and prevented stampedes and rustling. In 1885 one hundred cowboys, sixteen chuck-wagons (for provisions), and 500 saddle horses took part in a round-up of 60,000 cattle.

War broke out in 1914. Canada and Newfoundland sent more than 400,000 soldiers. Canadian troops withstood the first German gas attacks at Ypres, took part in the battle on the Somme River, and captured Vimy Ridge in northern France.

Sixty thousand were killed. Their gallantry was honoured by the building of the Peace Tower at Ottawa, and a monument on Vimy Ridge.

Canada had helped so much to win peace that it now became important in world affairs. Its representative signed the Peace Treaty. When the League of Nations was formed to prevent another world war, Canada became a member.

Without leaving the British Empire, Canada had become independent. In 1926 it was declared that part of the Empire was now the British Commonwealth of Nations, a group of equal and independent countries united by loyalty to the King. Since then the Commonwealth has grown and flourished. Today its members are Great Britain, Canada, Australia, New Zealand, the Union of South Africa, India, Pakistan, and Ceylon.

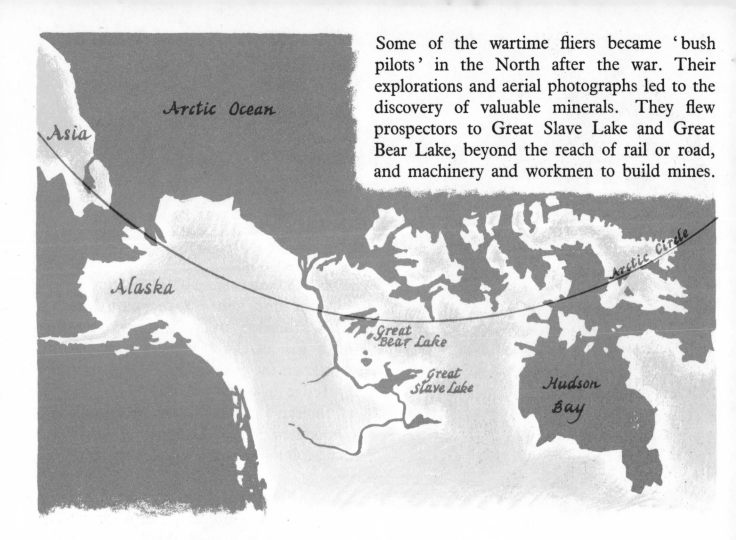

Some of the wartime fliers became 'bush pilots' in the North after the war. Their explorations and aerial photographs led to the discovery of valuable minerals. They flew prospectors to Great Slave Lake and Great Bear Lake, beyond the reach of rail or road, and machinery and workmen to build mines.

Today bush pilots watch for forest fires and carry freight between isolated mining towns like Yellowknife and the outside world.

At the University of Toronto Dr Frederick Banting and Dr Charles H. Best discovered insulin, which relieves diabetes.

A great Canadian painter, James Wilson Morrice, was working in Paris and the West Indies. Younger artists at home formed the Group of Seven and painted the rugged beauty of the Canadian North.

Industry flourished. The north country produced new goods that other countries wanted — woodpulp for making paper, and radium, more precious than gold. The world was Canada's market.

Suddenly the Great Depression came. Prices dropped in the world markets and trade almost halted. Factories closed their gates. Nearly half the working people were without jobs. On top of this, rain ceased to fall on the prairies. Crops dried up and the soil turned to dust.

The depression did not fully end until 1939 when war broke out. Then there was work for everyone as a steady stream of war materials flowed from Canada.

Over a million men and women served in the armed forces. The Royal Canadian Navy grew to be the third largest in the world. Flying schools across Canada trained airmen from all parts of the Commonwealth and from many other countries.

When the war ended in 1945 the new war-time industries and scientific discoveries were directed to the aims of peace. Uranium from Great Bear Lake gave scientists material for developing peaceful uses for atomic power. Newfoundland joined Canada in 1949. This newest province was really the oldest part of Canada, for its fisheries had brought the first adventurers from England, France, Spain, and Portugal.

The fishermen of New-foundland still put out to the Grand Banks, and others cross the Atlantic from Europe as their ancestors did 350 years ago. Each summer the brightly coloured sails of the Portuguese fishing fleet can be seen in the harbour of St John's. In Nova Scotia descendants of Scottish settlers hold gatherings where tartaned clansmen compete in Highland games and dances, The Gaelic language is often heard on Cape Breton Island.

In French-speaking Quebec the City Hall now stands where Louis Hébert first farmed the soil of New France. But outside the city, men still work the narrow farms laid out by Talon.

Where Maisonneuve planted his cross of wood three centuries ago a lighted cross shines at night over Montreal — next to Paris, the largest French-speaking city in the world.

The skyscrapers of Toronto tower over the busy harbour of what was once muddy York. Armed with rifles, Eskimos hunt caribou that move north in great herds each spring over the tundra of the Arctic barrens.

Across the wide prairie, the cowboys gather every year at the Calgary Stampede to display their skill in roping calves and riding wild steers.

Chuck-wagons pulled by four-horse teams thunder past the cheering crowd as they head for the finish line.

At the foot of the Coast Mountains the Port of Vancouver is crowded with fishing boats, freighters, and liners that voyage to the Orient.

The dream of the Fathers of Confederation has come true. A great nation, covering half a continent, stretches from sea to sea.

The pioneer past is close to Canadians. Now there is a challenge for modern pioneers. The cold North, the rough bush country, and the western mountains are yielding rich stores of minerals; their rushing rivers are making new electric power. No longer obstacles to the growth of the nation, these vast empty spaces are Canada's new frontier.

A MARI USQUE AD MARE

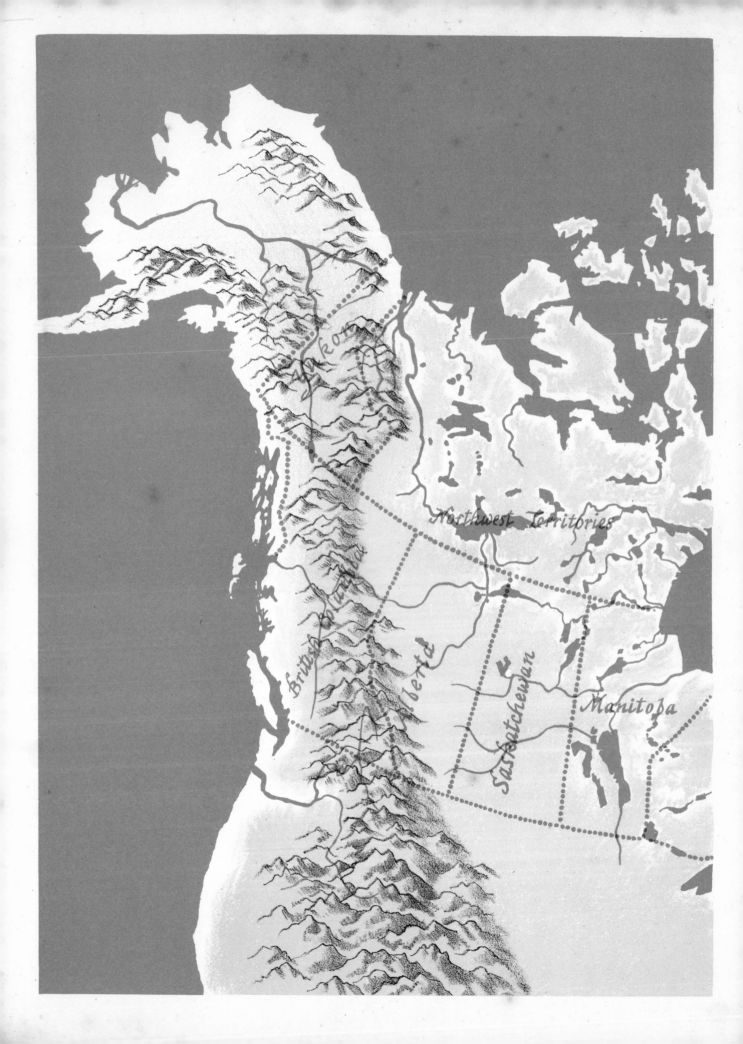